Symbols of Freedom

National Parks

Glacier National Park

M.C. Hall

Heinemann Library
Chicago, Illinois

Customer Service 888-454-2279
Visit our website at www.heinemannlibrary.com

Page layout by Richard Parker and Maverick Design
Photo research by Maria Joannou
Illustrations by Jeff Edwards
Printed and bound in China by South China Printing Company Limited

10 09 08 07 06
10 9 8 7 6 5 4 3 2 1

Library of Congress Cataloging-in-Publication Data
Hall, Margaret, 1947-
    Glacier National Park / Margaret Hall.
        p. cm. -- (National parks)
Includes bibliographical references and index.
ISBN 1-4034-6698-X (alk. paper) -- ISBN 1-4034-6705-6 (pbk. : alk. paper)
1. Glacier National Park (Mont.)--Juvenile literature. I. Title. II. Series.
    F737.G5H347 2005
    978.6'52034--dc22

                                    2004030474

Acknowledgments
The author and publishers are grateful to the following for permission to reproduce copyright material:
Alamy pp. **22**, **23** (Jeff Foott); Corbis pp. **11** (Michael S. Yamashita), **8** (Bettmann), **20** (Darrell Gulin), **21** (David Muench), **13**, **19** (Galen Rowell), **14** (Joel W Rogers), **4**, **10** (Layne Kennedy), **7**, **15**, **27** (Lowell Georgia), **5**, **26** (Steve Kaufman); Gibson Stock Photography p. **18**; Library of Congress p. **9**; Lonely Planet Images p. **16** (John Elk III 16); National Park Service pp. **12**, **17**, **29**, **30**, **31**, **32**; NHPA p. **24** (John Shaw); Photolibrary.com p. **25** (Oxford Scientific Films)

Cover photograph of Glacier National Park reproduced with permission of AGPix (Randy Beacham)

Some words are shown in bold, **like this**. You can find out what they mean by looking in the glossary.

Contents

Our National Parks

National parks are areas of land set aside for people to visit and enjoy **nature**. These parks do not belong to one person. They belong to everyone in the United States.

There are more than 50 national parks in the United States. Glacier National Park is one of the largest national parks. The park is named for its many **glaciers**.

A glacier is like a river of moving ice.

Glacier National Park

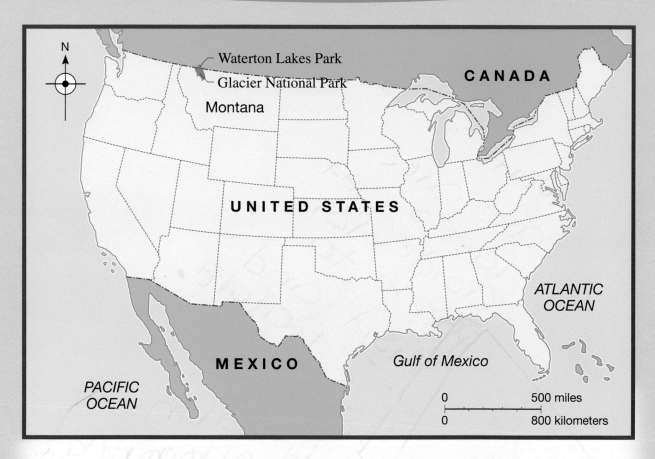

N

Waterton Lakes Park

Glacier National Park

Montana

CANADA

UNITED STATES

ATLANTIC
OCEAN

MEXICO

Gulf of Mexico

PACIFIC
OCEAN

| 0 | 500 miles |
| 0 | 800 kilometers |

Glacier National Park is in the western part of the United States. The park is located in northwestern Montana. Waterton Lakes National Park in **Canada** is north of Glacier.

Together, Glacier and Waterton are called Waterton-Glacier **International** Peace Park. This park stands for peace and understanding between the United States and Canada.

Glacier Long Ago

This Native American camp was on the shore of "Two Medicine Lake."

Native Americans were the first people to live in what is now Glacier National Park. They called the mountains of Glacier the "backbone of the world."

This picture shows George Grinnell and his wife Elizabeth standing on Grinnell Glacier in 1925.

Other people came to Glacier for gold, furs, and **lumber**. Then visitors came just to see the mountains. In 1910 the United States **government** made Glacier a **national park**.

Visiting Glacier National Park

Most people visit Glacier National Park in July and August, when it is warm. They camp, hike, fish, ride horseback, and go boating.

It usually starts to snow at Glacier in September. The snow often lasts until June. Winter visitors come to the park to ski or **snowshoe**.

Visitors can hike through the snow in Glacier National Park.

The Rocky Mountains

The Rocky Mountains run through Glacier National Park. Some of the mountains are very high. They are covered with snow all year.

Cimbers use special equipment to reach high peaks.

Some people come to Glacier National Park to climb the mountains. Climbers who reach the top get wonderful views of the park.

Glaciers

There are more than 50 **glaciers** in the park. The glaciers form when so much snow falls that it does not all melt during the summer.

Boats carry people across lakes to trails that lead to glaciers.

Because glaciers move so slowly, people can walk on some of them.

The snow piles up in thick layers. Then it starts moving down the mountain. A glacier only moves a few feet in a whole year.

# Going-to-the-Sun Road

Most visitors travel through the park on Going-to-the-Sun Road. The road runs along the sides of the mountains. In some places it is very steep.

It took eleven years to build the Going-to-the-Sun Road.

Going-to-the-Sun Road closes in the fall
when it starts to snow. The road does
not open again until late spring, when plows
can clear away the snow.

Lakes and Waterfalls

There are many beautiful lakes in Glacier National Park. Visitors fish and go boating on the lakes. The water is usually too cold for swimming!

Lake McDonald is the largest lake in the park.

The park also has many waterfalls. Some waterfalls form when rivers tumble over the edges of high **cliffs**, which are on the sides of mountains.

Park Plants

Most of Glacier National Park is covered with thick forests of hemlock, cedar, and pine trees. There are also large **meadows** filled with tall grasses.

Trees do not grow in the highest parts of the park. Beautiful wildflowers like glacier lilies and mountain pinks grow where trees cannot.

Park Animals

Visitors often see deer, moose, and elk. Mountain lions and wolves hunt for these animals. They also hunt smaller animals like rabbits, marmots, and squirrels.

hoary marmot

Bald eagles often live high in the mountains. Sometimes visitors spot eagle nests in the trees. Birds like hawks, loons, ducks, and owls are also common.

This bald eagle has caught a fish.

Mountain goats have hooves that bend to help them hold onto the rocks.

Mountain goats and bighorn sheep live on the steep mountainsides. Visitors sometimes see these animals jumping from rock to rock.

The park is home to many black bears and grizzly bears. People must stay away from these dangerous animals.

grizzly bear

Park People

Park rangers work at visitor centers and other places around the park. They lead hikes and teach visitors about the park's plants and animals.

Native Americans also give talks to park
visitors. They tell about the people who lived
in the area long ago. Visitors can also see
Native American dances.

Map of Glacier National Park

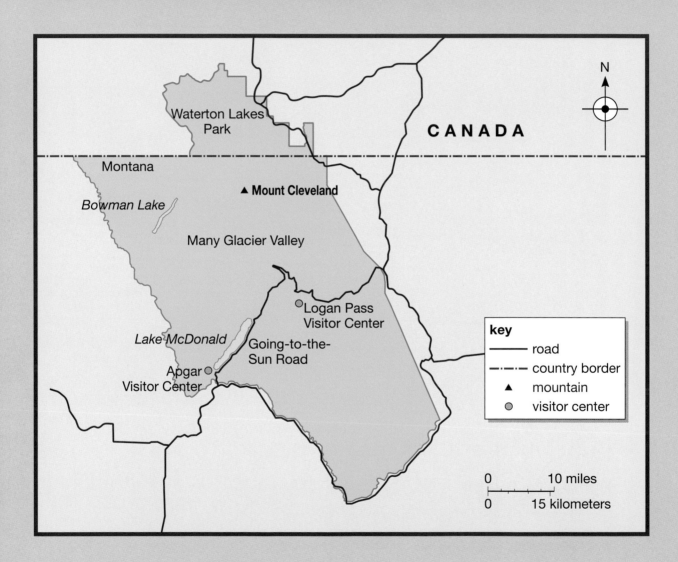

Waterton Lakes Park

CANADA

N

Montana

Bowman Lake

▲ **Mount Cleveland**

Many Glacier Valley

○Logan Pass Visitor Center

Lake McDonald

Going-to-the-Sun Road

Apgar Visitor Center

key

――― road

―·―·― country border

▲ mountain

○ visitor center

0   10 miles

0   15 kilometers

Timeline

1800s	English, French, and Spanish trappers come to Glacier to trap beaver
1891	The Great Northern Railway reaches Glacier. Visitors begin coming to the area.
1895	The United States **government** buys part of Glacier from the Blackfeet tribe. Miners come in search of gold and copper.
1900	Glacier becomes a Forest Preserve
1910	Glacier is set aside as a **national park**
1921	Work begins on Going-to-the-Sun Road
1932	Going-to-the-Sun Road is completed
1932	Glacier and Waterton Lakes in **Canada** become the world's first **International** Peace Park
1995	Glacier becomes a World Heritage Site

Glossary

Canada country that is north of the United States

cliffs high, steep areas of land

glacier large area of moving ice and snow

government group of people that makes laws for and runs a country

international belonging to or related to more than one country

lumber trees cut down so the wood can be used

meadow grassy field with few or no trees

national park natural area set aside by the government for people to visit

nature the outdoors and the wild plants and animals found there

park ranger man or woman who works in a national park and shares information about the wildlife and unusual sights of the park

snowshoe to travel on top of the snow on snowshoes that are attached to boots

# Find Out More

Books
An older reader can help you with these books:

Domeniconi, David. *M is for Majestic: A National Parks Alphabet.* Farmington Hills, Mich.: Gale Group, 2003.

Gilda, Robert. *Bighorn Sheep: Mountain Monarchs.* Minneapolis, Minn.: Econo-Clad Books, 2001.

Graf, Mike. *Glacier National Park.* Mankato, Minn.: Bridgestone Books, 2004.

Llewellyn, Claire. *Glaciers.* Chicago, Ill.: Heinemann Library, 2002.

Mader, Jan. *Rocky Mountains.* San Francisco, Calif.: Children's Press, 2004.

Raatma, Lucia. *Our National Parks.* Mankato, Minn.: Compass Point Books, 2002.

Address
To find out more about Glacier National Park, write to:

Glacier National Park
Park Headquarters
P.O. Box 128
West Glacier, MT 59936

Index